JANICE HARPER
32 WATERMILL WAY

GW01451810

SKETCHBOOK

OF

CREATIVITY

IN FLOWER DESIGN

JUNE ROBISON KAHL

Illustrated by
Ellen Parsons

PROSPECT HILL PRESS
Baltimore, Maryland

Acknowledgments

To those whose support and encouragement made this book possible.

To those who gave me cutting privileges in their gardens—Virginia Shure, Chris Armor, and Maria O'Rourk—and to Annette Richter for her driftwood.

To Thelma Bauer, florist, for her beautiful flowers and her willingness to go out of her way to acquire the plant material.

To Eleanor Heldrich, photographer, for capturing the excitement of creativity.

To Ellen Parsons, illustrator, for her artistic sketches and advice on all artistic decisions.

To the editor of the Prospect Hill Publishing Company for her invaluable editorial assistance.

To the members of my family for all their help in collecting the material for this book.

To the National Council of State Garden Clubs for providing the opportunity for me to become a Master Flower Show Judge.

Copyright © 1988 by June Robison Kahl

All rights reserved. No part of this publication may be reproduced, copied, or transmitted in any form or by any means, electronic, mechanical, photocopying, or otherwise without prior permission of Prospect Hill Press.

Library of Congress Catalog Card Number is 88-60177

ISBN 0-941526-06-2

Published by Prospect Hill Press
216 Wendover Road
Baltimore, Maryland 21218

Dedicated to my husband, George, and children, June, George, and Stuart.

TABLE OF CONTENTS

INTRODUCTION

Creativity is the ability to use one's imagination to create beauty, joy, and humor. Creativity is limited only by one's imagination. This book will endeavor to teach the techniques needed to transform imagination into reality. The home, the garden, and the flower show are three of the sites in which to express creativity with flowers and other plant material.

The fundamentals of the art of creating designs with plant material are taught in my first book, **A Sketchbook of Easy Flower Designs**. Design elements, the basic visual qualitites of a design, are space, line, form, size, color, texture, pattern, and light. These elements are used according to the design principles of balance, proportion, scale, rhythm, dominance, and contrast. The directions for making the basic designs in the first book give definite heights and sizes for the plant material and definite instructions for placement. However, as the arranger progresses to this book, while still adhering to the basic elements and principles of good design, more freedom in choosing containers and plant material is stressed. The arranger is encouraged to experiment with unusual containers and plant material, using this book as a guide for creativity and freedom of expression.

Decorating the home is an important concern in modern day living. Flowers and plants create an aura of beauty when they become a part of the decor. Every meal, every day, every season, and every occasion can be the inspiration to be creative. Houseplants can be a good source of foliage for flower arranging. Select plants for their foliage and color, or for the size and shape of their leaves. Unusual foliage adds interest to florist flowers.

Landscaping the garden is the art of improving the land for use and enjoyment. A garden or patio is an outdoor living area used for relaxing, dining, and recreation. Don't overlook the out-of-doors as a place in which to be creative. The most important consideration in creating a large sculpture for the garden is the suitability of the object to its place in the landscape. There should be a blending of the sculpture with the natural beauty of the garden.

A flower show is a very good place in which to display creativity. It provides the setting and creates the atmosphere for one's imagination to experiment with color and techniques, and to try the different, the unusual, and the extreme in containers, flowers, and interpretation of theme. Originality is the stimulant that helps to create beauty.

The purpose of this book is to stimulate creativity in its readers and to provide the techniques and procedures by which to achieve it.

June R. Kahl

Baltimore, Maryland

FUNDAMENTALS OF FLOWER ARRANGING

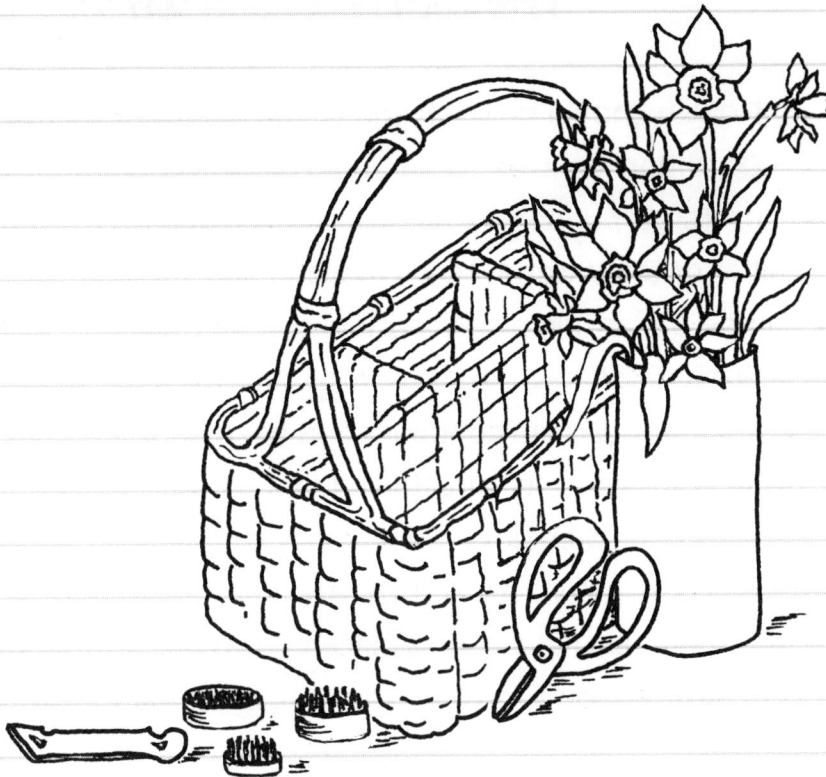

FLOWER ARRANGER'S WORKBASKET

A flower arranger is an artist working with live plant material; and, like every artist, he or she will need some basic tools and equipment. Keeping everything together in one place, ready to use, is the function of an arranger's workbasket. It should include:

1. Flower scissors with sharp, straight blades—to cut stems so they can absorb water easily.

2. Needlepoint holders and needlepoint pincups—to hold flowers.

3. Floral clay—to attach needlepoint holders to containers.

4. Floral foam—to hold flowers in containers when needlepoint holders cannot be used.

5. Can opener—to remove needlepoint holders from containers.

6. Floral wire of medium gauge (#20)—to hold plant material in place.

7. Tall container—for water to condition flowers.

PREPARATION OF PLANT MATERIAL

1. Flowers should be fresh and at the height of their perfection.

2. Condition all flowers immediately by cutting off at least one inch of stem, preferably under water. Strip off bottom leaves and place in a deep container of tepid water. Leave in water several hours or overnight to harden before arranging. Exception: daffodils require shallow water.

3. Wash all foliage to remove dust. Remove broken or damaged leaves.

4. Start with a clean container and needlepoint holder.

5. Sit with container directly in front of you.

6. Attach needlepoint holder to dry container.

7. Fill container with water before you start to make a design.

8. Remember that the first placement is the most important. Select the most beautiful and the strongest of the plant material marked in each design for #1.

9. Supplies may be purchased from florist or garden center.

TO ATTACH A NEEDLEPOINT HOLDER

1. To attach a needlepoint holder to a dry container, first roll a piece of floral clay, between both hands, into a long, slender, cigarette shape.

2. Attach this roll of clay to the outer edge of an upside down needlepoint holder, making sure you join the two ends of clay together.

3. Place the needlepoint holder in the container and press down hard, giving it a slight twist. This will create suction, which holds the needlepoint holder in place.

TO BEND FRESH PLANT MATERIAL

1. Start halfway up stem.

2. Place both thumbs touching underneath stem with other fingers over top of stem.

3. Gently apply pressure.

4. Keep applying pressure while moving fingers up to end of branch.

5. Repeat this procedure until the stem is bent as much as desired.

6. To make a loop, bring tip around until it crosses main stem. Cut a 1 1/2" piece of medium-gauge florist wire. Bend the piece of wire around the main stem and the tip of the plant material. Each turn of the wire should be as neat and close together as possible. Do not twist wire— simply bend it around the stems.

SECTION I

DESIGNS FOR THE HOME

Flowers bring beauty and joy to a home. Each room can become the setting for a different style or type of flower design. Give imagination and ingenuity free rein to make use of the colors and shapes of flowers and foliage, whether they come from the garden or the florist.

The satisfaction of creating with flowers is never-ending. Each container filled with flowers becomes an object of beauty—a piece of living art. Anything that holds water can become a container. Holidays and special occasions become outstanding and memorable when flowers, fruit, and evergreens are used profusely in the home.

This design for the hall was inspired by the architecture of the Opera House in Sydney, Australia. In selecting the plant material—Yucca leaves—only the tallest and largest leaves were used. The narrow triangular container needed only two needlepoint holders, but a narrow oval or rectangular container would require three. Any large flowers could be used, such as Dahlia, Peony, or Chrysanthemum.

SUPPLIES

    Container—Japanese long narrow
       triangle
    2 needlepoint holders—approxi-
       mately 3″ long by 1″ wide

PLANT MATERIAL

    6 Yucca leaves
    2 Chrysanthemum flowers—large

PROCEDURE

Place one needlepoint holder against the back right side of the container and the second one slightly to the left of center.

Insert the three largest Yucca leaves—#1, #2, and #3—as close together as possible on the right needlepoint holder.

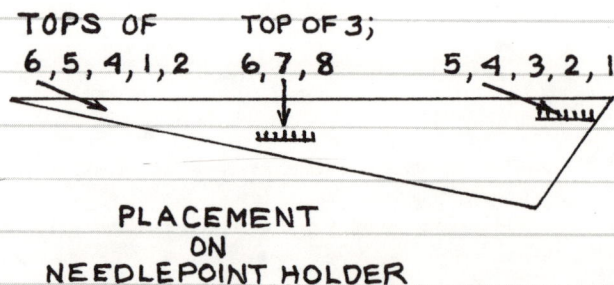

TOPS OF   TOP OF 3;
6,5,4,1,2   6,7,8   5,4,3,2,1

PLACEMENT
ON
NEEDLEPOINT HOLDER

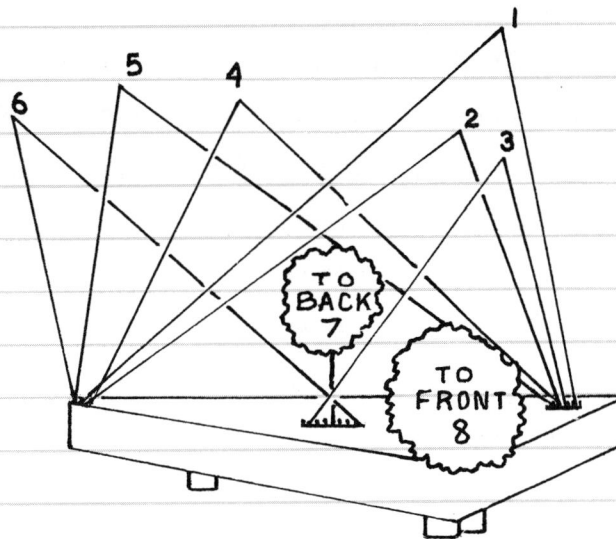

Bend #1 and #2 until their tops touch the extreme left side of the container. Each leaf should be bent at a slightly different height to create different angles. The narrow point of the container will hold the Yucca tops in place. (If an oval or rectangular container is used, there will need to be an additional needlepoint placed on the left side to hold the tops.) Lean #1 slightly toward the back and #2 slightly toward the front.

Bend #3 until the top can be inserted on the center needlepoint holder.

Insert #4 and #5 close to #3 and bend their tops until they touch the extreme left side of the container, creating slightly different angles.

Place #6 on the center needlepoint and bend until top touches the left side of container.

Place #7 flower on center needlepoint holder and slant to back.

Place #8 flower on center needlepoint holder and slant to front.

NOTE: This design depends upon the interesting spaces created by the different angles of the bent leaves. Each leaf is bent at a different point along its length, and not all of the leaves are bent straight across. #1, #4, #5, #6, and #7 lean to the back and #2, #3, and #8 lean to the front.

DESIGN 2   LIVING ROOM

Two kinds of dried plant material were used in a large, orange Japanese container. No mechanics were necessary because of the small opening in the top of the container, which was completely filled with the branches and flowers. The Paulownia tomentosa is a deciduous Chinese tree with thick, stiff branches, which grows to a height of fifty feet. It is sometimes called the Empress Tree. Chinese Puzzle is a spiky, dried weed that can be purchased at a florist or garden shop, and Liatris is a showy perennial herb whose blooms are predominantly rose-purple.

SUPPLIES

    Container—Japanese tall orange

    Florist wire

PLANT MATERIAL

    3 Paulownia branches—dried

    10 Liatris—purple

    4 Chinese Puzzle stems—dried

PROCEDURE

Place the tallest Paulownia branch (#1) upright in the container. To enhance the line created by the plant material, a slightly shorter branch (#2) is wired upside down to #1. Branch #2 sweeps across the front of the container from right to left. To reinforce this line, if desired, another short branch (#3) may be wired to branch #2, following the line of branch #2.

16

In the top of the container, place the 4 stems (#4, #5, #6, #7) of Chinese Puzzle, each approximately 8″ to 10″ long. Then add the pieces of purple Liatris to make a sunburst effect together with the Chinese puzzle.

To add interest to the design, the opening in the center of the container was left empty.

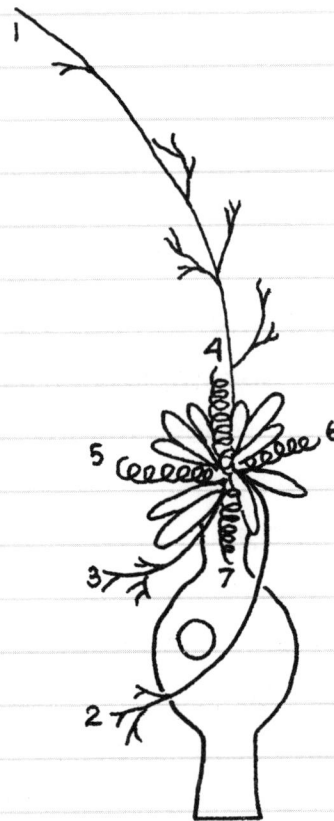

DESIGN 3   DINING ROOM

A Chinese bowl used with a carved wooden base makes an attractive container for a fruit centerpiece. Oranges were used for the design pictured here because they picked up the orange color in the bowl. To soften the orange color, half of the Oranges were studded with whole cloves. This also added variety to the design and aroma to the fruit. Sprigs of Pyracantha berries were used to fill in the spaces between the Oranges; however, Rose hips or Boxwood could be substituted for the Pyracantha.

SUPPLIES

    Container—Chinese bowl (10″
        diameter) and wooden base
    Green styrofoam cone—12″ high
    Round wooden toothpicks
    Whole cloves

PLANT MATERIAL

    24 Oranges—medium size
    Pyracantha berry sprigs

PREPARATION

A day ahead cut the berry sprigs and stand them in water until ready to use. Cut off the top 1 1/2″ of the styrofoam cone, then attach the base of the cone to the bowl with floral clay or floral adhesive tape. Stud one Orange completely with cloves; this Orange is to be used for the top of the design. Half of the remaining Oranges should be studded with cloves on one side only.

ALWAYS start building this design from the bottom and work upward. Around the cone, arrange a ring of Oranges to rest on the rim of the container. Place the Oranges so they are spaced evenly with no large gaps between the fruit. Alternate plain Oranges with the clove-studded ones.

PROCEDURE

ROW 1—Remove one Orange and put two toothpicks, about 1/2″ apart, at that place in the cone. Then impale the Orange on the toothpicks. Repeat this step until there is a complete circle of Oranges around the cone.

ROW 2—Place this row of Oranges so each piece of fruit rests above the space between the Oranges in the row below, alternating the plain and the clove-studded ones. Attach in the same manner as Row 1.

ROW 3 and 4—Attach the remaining Oranges in the same manner, continuing to alternate the plain and the clove-studded ones.

TOP OF CONE—In the center of the flat surface where the cone top was cut, place three toothpicks in a triangle 1/2″ apart. Impale the completely clove-studded Orange on these toothpicks.

Insert small sprigs of Pyracantha berries in all the small spaces between the oranges, being careful not to cover too much of the fruit.

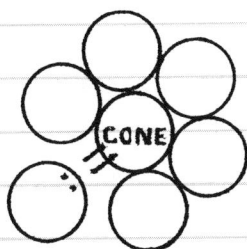

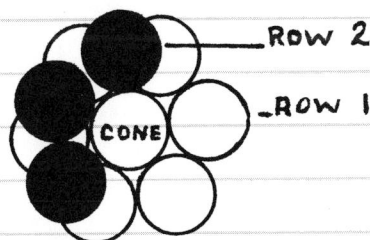

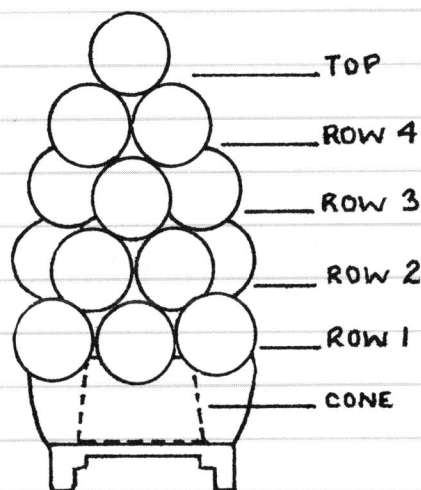

DESIGN 4   DEN

The coffee table in the den is used as the setting for a brass fish dish and tray from Persia. Because of the unusual shape of the container, green Bells of Ireland were selected for the plant material. Their distinctive form and pattern, as well as their graceful poses, enhance the shape of the container. Also, the design is free-standing (seen from all sides), and Bells of Ireland do not have a back or a front; they are the same on all sides. Purple Statice was used as the filler plant material to add contrast to the design.

SUPPLIES

    Container—Brass fish dish and

        tray from Persia

    Needlepoint holder—long rec-

        tangle, 2″ by 4″

PLANT MATERIAL

    6 Bells of Ireland

    6 Statice—purple

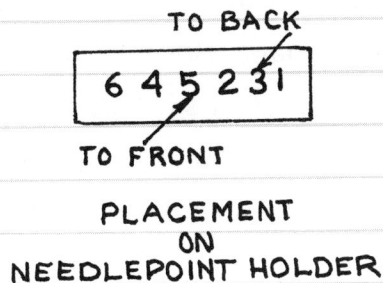

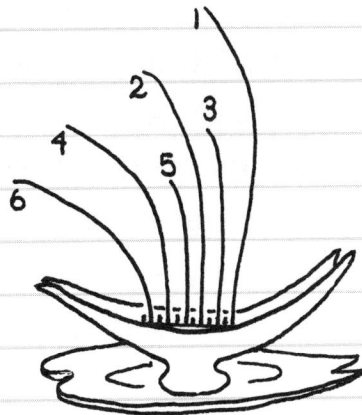

TO BACK

6	4	5	2	3	1

TO FRONT

PLACEMENT
ON
NEEDLEPOINT HOLDER

PROCEDURE

To give the Bells of Ireland a neat look, trim off the top of each flower and remove all the small leaves. Using the tallest flower as a guide, cut each one shorter than the proceeding one. To do this, lay all the flowers down on a table. Arrange them with their tops in descending order, their stems sticking out over the edge of the table. Cut their stems even with the table's edge. Then, picking up each one in order (#1 to #6), place them on a needlepoint holder.

Place the tallest Bells of Ireland, #1, to the extreme right of container.

Place #2, #4, and #6 in an orderly fashion from right to left.

Place #3 to the back between #1 and #2.

Place #5 to the front between #2 and #4.

Statice is placed in and around the Bells of Ireland, but it should be only half as tall. Start with the tallest Statice and place it to the extreme right, working toward the left.

VARIATION: For a fall design, substitute Eucalyptus for Bells of Ireland.

DESIGN 5   BEDROOM

A dried, mass flower design is delightful when used on a night table in a bedroom. A small pitcher decorated with a hunt scene was used as a container for the design in the photograph. Lunaria (Honesty), an herb of the mustard family, was selected to create the mass. Its luminous quality gives a light, airy feeling to the design. To pick up the color of the hunt coats on the pitcher, small dried red Chrysanthemums from the garden were used.

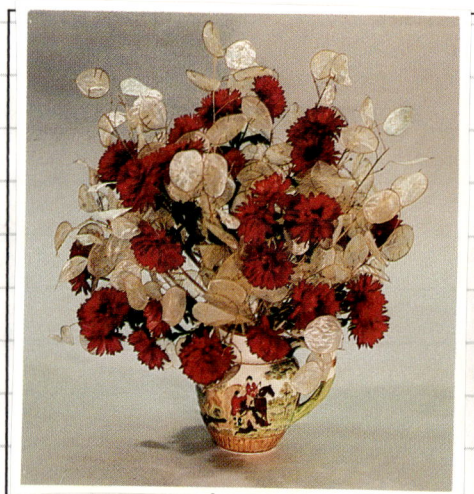

SUPPLIES

    Container—English pitcher 5″

     high

    Floral foam

PLANT MATERIAL

    12 Lunaria—dried

    16 Chrysanthemum sprays with

     small red flowers—dried

PREPARATION

Each parchment-like pod of the Lunaria plant is made of three parts. Place each pod between the thumb and first finger and gently rub, taking care not to tear or break the pod. The two outer shells and the black seeds will fall off. What remains is a satiny paper-like oval. Lunaria is a very attractive plant for use in dried winter designs.

PROCEDURE

Fill pitcher with dry floral foam.

Cut #1 Lunaria nine inches long and place in the center.

Cut #2, #3, and #4 seven inches long and place around #1.

Cut #5, #6, and #7 five inches long and place around #2, #3, and #4.

Cut #8, #9, and #10 four inches long and place around #5, #6, and #7.

Cut #11 and #12 four inches long and place where needed to fill out the mass.

Place the flowers throughout the Lunaria, each at a different height.

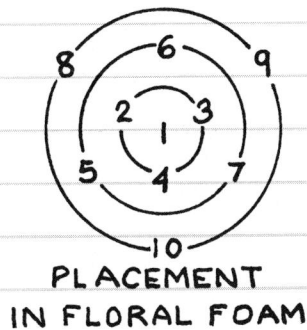

PLACEMENT
IN FLORAL FOAM

- - - - TO BACK
_____ TO FRONT

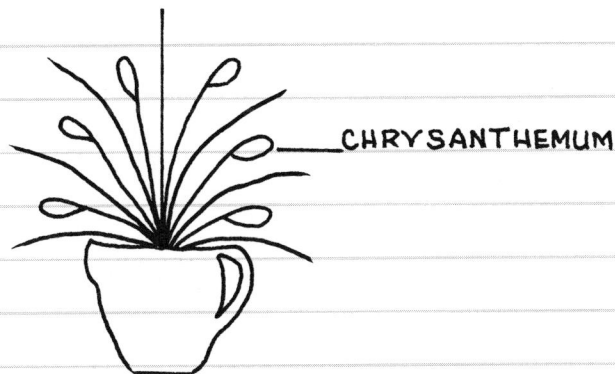

CHRYSANTHEMUM

SECTION II

DESIGNS FOR THE GARDEN AND PATIO

Both garden and patio offer novel locations in which to express creativity. Large garden sculptures, with or without added flowers, can add interest and excitement to the landscape. Making a wood or stone sculpture offers a creative outlet for originality and imagination.

Weathered wood is that which has been exposed to the weather, namely sun, rain, and wind. Driftwood is that which has been washed by the ocean, lake, or stream.

Driftwood with sculptural qualities of curves, circles, straight lines, and rounded and flat areas makes unusual natural sculptures that can be used in the garden the entire year. Driftwood is just as interesting in winter with snow as it is in summer with flowers. Sculptural pieces can be made to any size or height by nailing smaller pieces together.

Creating flower designs with lava or featherstone containers can be fun. A piece of stone sculpture is always appropriate for use in the garden.

Driftwood used on a patio dining table becomes a conversation piece. A patio, porch, or balcony is also the perfect setting for a naturalistic-looking mobile made of small pieces of wood with knotholes.

DESIGN 6   WOOD SCULPTURE

A driftwood sculpture is very decorative inside as well as outside the home. Half the fun of collecting driftwood is being able to display it. A wood sculpture can be placed on a table in the hall, on the floor beside the fireplace, or on a coffee table. Size will dictate which location would be appropriate.

A piece of driftwood mounted on a base can be left in its natural state, or a highly-stylized design can be created by sanding and applying a finish.

In a modern home, black lacquer paint might be used to finish a driftwood sculpture; in a traditional home, wood stain and floor wax could be applied. For drama in a summer home, paint the sculpture either white or a bright color.

For a seaside setting, shells or brain coral could be used instead of flowers to decorate the driftwood. To make the shells more flower-like, wires wrapped with green corsage tape could be used as stems. Many shells and pieces of coral have the same shapes and forms as flowers.

SUPPLIES

Driftwood

Wood cube—5″ or 6″ square

Metal rod—1/4″ diameter

Drill

PLANT MATERIAL

6 Sterlitza leaves—dried

2 Allium flowers—large, dried

DRIFTWOOD —

METAL RODS —

WOOD BASE —

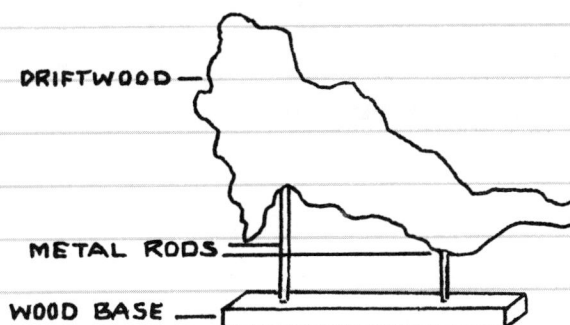

CONSTRUCTION

Scrub driftwood with a brush and let it dry. Drill a hole in the center of the wooden cube and insert the metal rod. The rod must be strong enough to support the piece of driftwood. Determine the best position or angle for the wood by moving it about, then mark on it the place where the hole for the rod should be drilled.

IMPORTANT: Make sure the wood is properly balanced on the rod. It should be firm and secure.

PROCEDURE

The wood sculpture can be used just as it is, or flowers and foliage may be wired onto it to enhance the shape of the wood. For the design in the photograph, dried flowers and foliage were wired to the wood.

If fresh flowers are used they must have a source of water. There are many ways of doing this. Waterpicks can be used, or a needepoint cup-holder can be wired to the wood. Or, a piece of wet floral foam can be covered with green florist foil and wired to the wood. Then, with a pencil, the foil can be pierced wherever plant material is to be inserted.

Arrange flowers and foliage in a free-style design to follow the lines of the weathered wood and to create a graceful, free-flowing effect.

VARIATION: Place the driftwood in a horizontal position as shown in the final sketch, using two or more rods for support.

DESIGN 7   LARGE DRIFTWOOD

A large piece of driftwood in the garden is always eye-catching. It is a wonderful accent piece and makes a beautiful container for flowers. The piece in the photograph is nearly 30" tall.

Co-ordinate the flowers added to the driftwood with the flowers used on the patio table. It can be the talk of a party. Place the driftwood in the garden where it can be seen from inside, and change the flowers as the season changes. For holiday spirit at Christmastime, have fun wiring Holly and a large red bow to the wood, and hope for a white Christmas.

SUPPLIES

Driftwood—large

Pincup—large

Saw

PLANT MATERIAL

3 Azalea branches

PROCEDURE

Scrub driftwood with a brush and let dry. Saw off the bottom evenly so the wood will stand erect. Place a pincup in the center of the wood and wire it in place so the wind will not dislodge it.

Select three beautiful branches of flowering azalea from the garden.

Place one piece on the left, one to the right, and one in the center of

PLACEMENT
ON
NEEDLEPOINT HOLDER

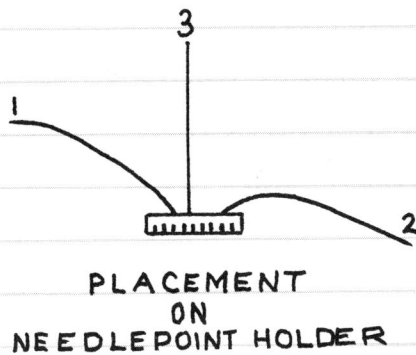

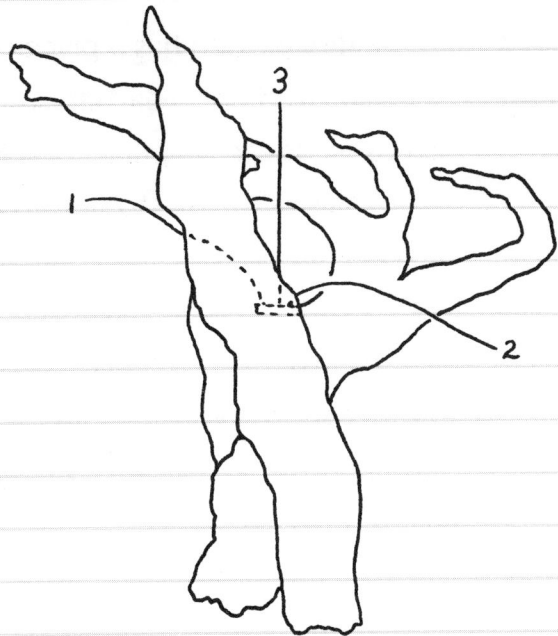

the pincup. To insert plant material with thick, woody stems on a needle-point, cut the bottoms straight across and place upright on the holder. Press the stems down firmly on the needles. Then, to force the stems to slant in the desired direction, place thumb against the bottom of the stem and press in the direction of the slant. Support the branch with one hand at the top while pressing with thumb at the bottom. The center stem is added last to allow space in which to work. This is a quick and easy way to add color to the driftwood.

The plant material used in the photograph was the Glendale Azalea 'Martha Hitchcock.'

VARIATIONS: Use a large piece of driftwood in place of a birdbath or in the center of an herb garden.

DESIGN 8   FEATHERSTONE SCULPTURE

Every garden has a place for a decorative stone whether it is natural or a sculptured one. Featherstone, or lavastone, is very lightweight and easy to carve. It can be purchased from a garden center.

The size of the stone purchased will be dictated by how it is to be used in the garden. The shape of featherstone can be changed easily by chiseling it with a few basic tools.

Weather will not damage the stone sculpture when it is placed in the garden. In the winter, snow will completely change the look of it. When adding flowers to a stone sculpture, use large flowers so that they can be seen from a distance.

SUPPLIES

　　Featherstone purchased from a
　　　garden center

　　Garden gloves

　　Hammer

　　Chisel

　　Pincups

PLANT MATERIAL

　　3 Fuji Chrysanthemums—yellow

　　5 Aspidistra leaves

PROCEDURE

To keep from getting minute cuts, always wear gloves while handling the stone. Determine the most interesting position for the stone, then chisel off a flat bottom surface so it can stand firmly on the ground. Enjoy yourself by hammering and chiseling out holes, angles, and places for the

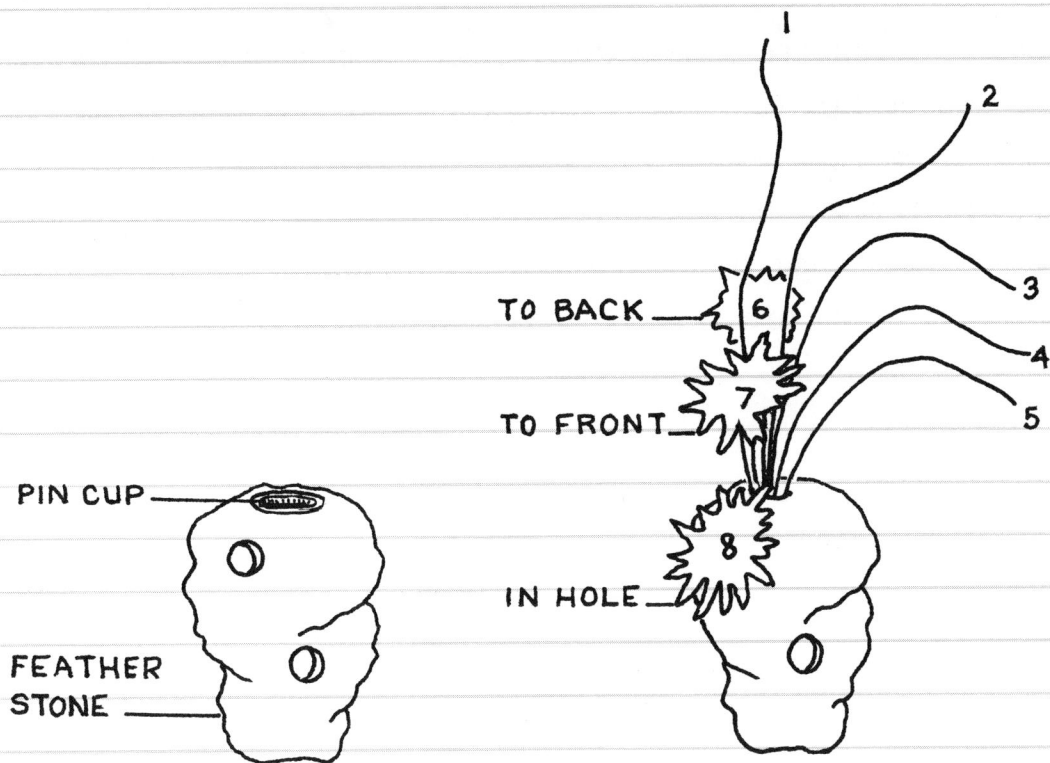

pincups. Light, coming through holes chiseled completely through the stone, adds sparkle to the design. Shape the surface of the stone with ridges and indentations to make it more interesting.

Insert a pincup in the top hole and place the five Aspidistra leaves in the pincup in an orderly manner.

Start with leaf #1 to the left and standing upright. Working from left to right, place #2, #3, #4, and #5 each to the right of the preceding leaf and each slanting more to the right.

Flower #6 is placed to the rear upper left and flower #7 low and to the front. Put flower #8 in a small pincup in the hole in the center of the featherstone.

VARIATION: In place of large leaves, use any graceful flowering branch and omit the flowers. Example: Spirea 'Van Houttei'.

DESIGN 9   DRIFTWOOD AND CONTAINER

An unusual effect is achieved by combining driftwood with a container. If the container has several openings, it is easy to attach a piece of wood in one of the openings and plant material in the others. Select a piece of driftwood that adds to the look of the container. Place a small branch of the driftwood in an opening and wire it in place for stability. Contrasting textures, such as the smooth surface of a container and rough-textured wood, add interest to the design.

SUPPLIES

    Container with several

      openings—18″ tall

    Driftwood

PLANT MATERIAL

    5 Gladiolus—red

PREPARATION

    Condition the flowers by allowing them to stand in tepid water for several hours or, better still, overnight.

    Attach a piece of driftwood to the opening in the front of the container.

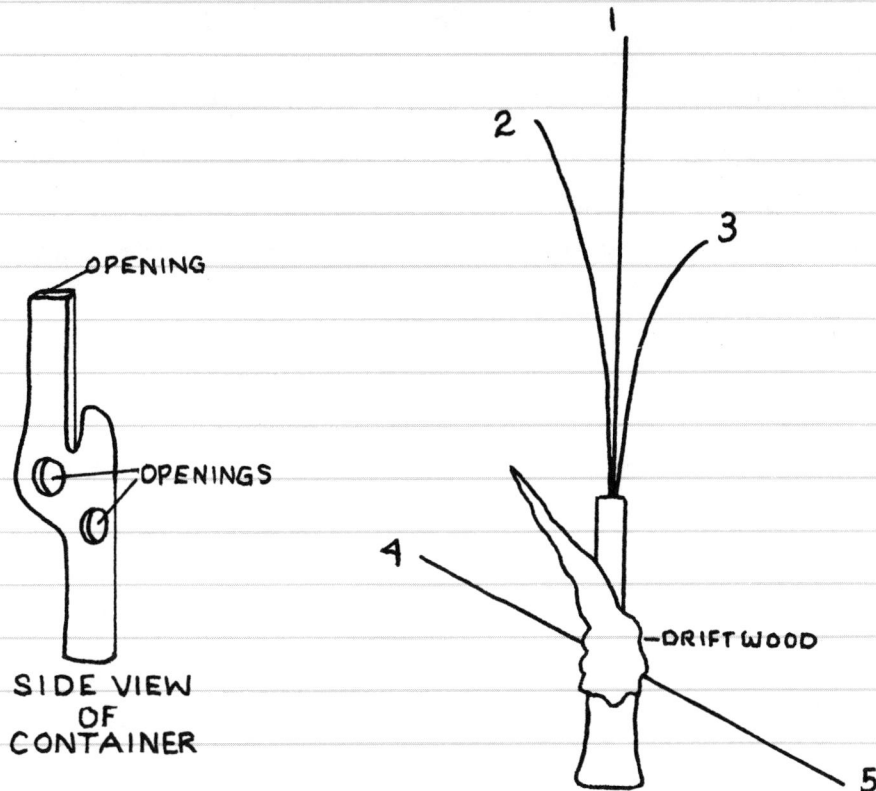

OPENING

OPENINGS

SIDE VIEW
OF
CONTAINER

DRIFTWOOD

PROCEDURE

Snap off the small top buds on each flower. Since this is a vertical design, the flowers should be tall and straight. Always exaggerate the height of a vertical design. Place Gladiolus #1, #2, and #3 in the top opening. Cut each one slightly shorter than the preceeding one. Place #1 in the center back, #2 to the left of #1 and slightly forward, and #3 to the right of #1 and slightly forward of #2. This is called the "shoelacing" method of placing plant material in a vertical design.

Create a diagonal line with the two remaining flowers by placing them in the opening in the container behind the wood. Flower #4 is placed on left side and slanting upward, while flower #5 is placed on the right side slanting down.

NOTE: This same piece of driftwood was used as the main support of the mobile in Design 10.

DESIGN 10   KNOTHOLE MOBILE

The mobile is an art form made of moving parts suspended from above. In constructing a mobile of natural material, the most important principle of design is balance. There are two kinds of balance.

1. Symmetrical balance—equal weight on each side of a real or imaginary axis.

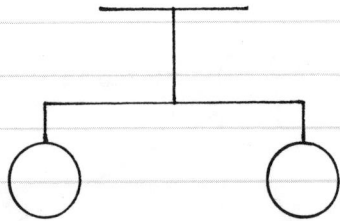

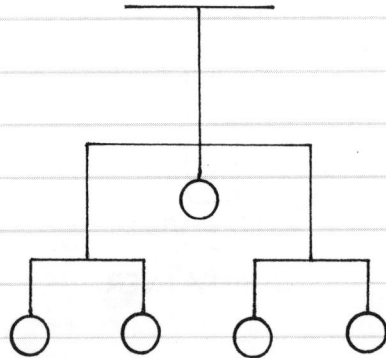

2. Assymmetrical balance—approximately equal visual weight composed of different elements on each side of a vertical axis.

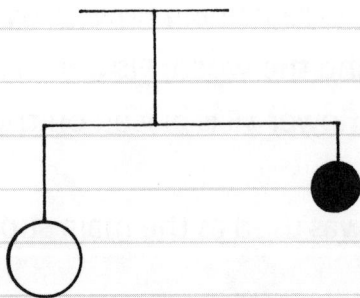

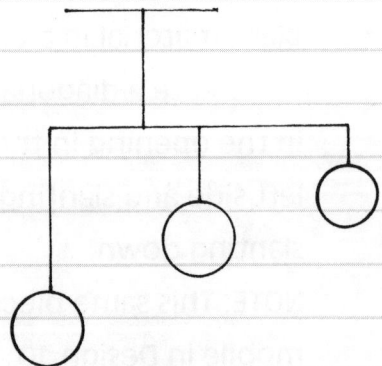

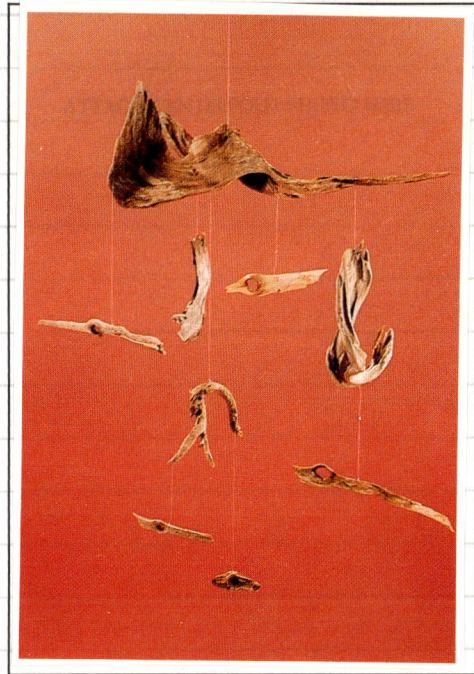

SUPPLIES

Nylon fishline

Small swivel

Drill

PLANT MATERIAL

1 Piece of weathered wood—
approximately 15″ long

8 Pieces of weathered wood with
knotholes—from 2″ to 6″ long

PROCEDURE

Plan the design of this mobile by placing the pieces of wood on a table in a pattern that is interesting. This design has three rows of wood pieces— first, one large piece of wood; then five small pieces; and, finally, three smaller pieces.

Hold the center top of the large piece of driftwood between the thumb and first finger. Move the fingers backwards and forwards until the wood is balanced so it will hang in a horizontal position. Drill a small hole at the exact spot in the wood where the fingers were holding it. Attach a long piece of fishline to the wood and suspend it, at eye level, from a door-way or clothes rack.

Drill a small hole through the top of each small piece of wood and tie a 20″ length of fishline to each piece.

Select the five pieces of wood that are to be tied, temporarily, to the top of the large piece of wood. Adjustments may be needed until the proper balance is achieved by moving the fishlines backwards and forwards, up and down. When the balance is found, mark the spots on the large piece of wood where the lines should be attached and drill a small hole at each mark. Carefully tie the small pieces of wood to the large piece. Do not cut off the excess fishline. More adjustments may be needed.

The three remaining pieces of wood are attached to the first row of wood using the same method for finding the balance.

Remove the fishline from the top of the large piece of wood and attach a swivel. Then attach the fishline to the swivel. Cut off all excess fishline. NOTE: All parts of the mobile should swing freely around each other. Adjust the length of the fishlines to achieve this freedom of movement.

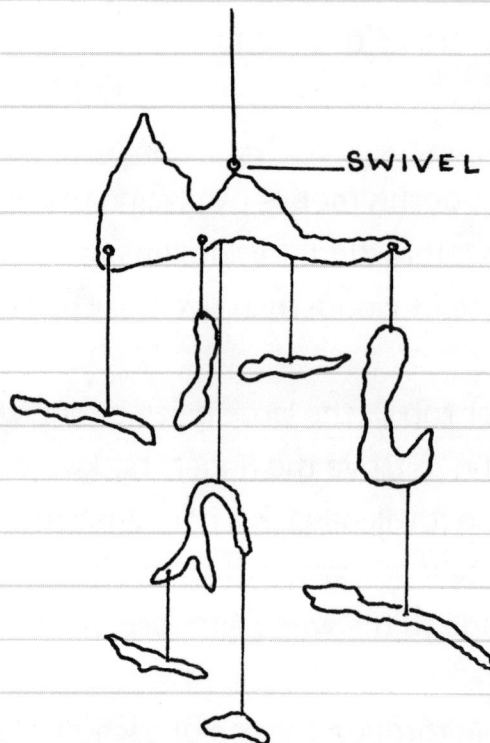

SWIVEL

SECTION III

DESIGNS FOR A FLOWER SHOW

A flower show is the place where both the gardener and the floral designer have an opportunity to display horticultural and artistic ability. The purpose of a flower show is to educate the public, to stimulate an interest in horticulture, and to serve as an outlet for creative expression. These shows may be sponsored by a single garden club, a group of clubs, a plant society, or any organized group such as a service club, department store, county fair, etc. They may be open to the public free of charge or a fee may be charged for admission.

The National Council of State Garden Clubs is an organization of state garden clubs whose members often co-sponsor shows with other organizations. Flower shows are staged in many places: churches, schools, armories, banks, museums, or indeed any place that is large enough, well-lighted, with ample parking, and convenient for exhibitors. These shows may be judged by accredited National Council Flower Show Judges who have successfully completed the requirements of five Flower Show Schools.

Participating in a flower show offers the opportunity to enjoy the beauty of plant material, to see innovative staging, and to learn gardening techniques. It is a chance to enter into the fun and experience of competing for ribbons and awards.

The flower show schedule is the law of the show and governs all aspects of it. It is the source of all necessary information about the show for the exhibitors and judges, and it serves as a guide for visitors. The requirements for each class clearly state the type of design that should be entered, the flowers that will be allowed, how the class will be staged, and the awards to be given.

An exhibitor should first read through the entire schedule then go back and reread the portions about those sections or classes that seemed interesting and sparked the imagination. Sometimes the starting place is a flower, sometimes a container, a theme, or an idea. Plant material may be fresh, dried, fresh and dried, or treated dried plant material.

The designs in the section that follows are the results of the author's own interpretations of a flower show schedule. They are meant to be a guide in planning and executing a design. Each one suggests a way to begin; that is, with a color, a flower, a container, or an idea. Each individual flower and each container may suggest a different way it might be used.

It is a question of visualizing an idea and then sketching it. Think about the shapes and colors of all the components and the best way to organize them into a flower design. Combining colors is an art in itself, as is combining the different flower shapes—round, oval, or spike.

Experimenting is essential in working out a creative design. Merely inserting a single branch in a container may suggest where the flowers should be placed. The spaces created by placing each branch are very important in determining the placement of the rest of the plant material.

In the Design Division of a flower show, which is the section of the show that exhibits the flower designs, it is required that all plant material be listed correctly on a card that is placed with the design. In the Horticulture Division, where plant specimens are displayed, the entries, in order to be eligible for a Top Honor Ribbon, must be labeled with the correct botanical name—that is, genus, species, and/or variety/cultivar.

DESIGN 11   BEGIN WITH A FLOWER

Class 1. A free-form design of all fresh plant material.

If the decision to enter a flower show begins with the desire to use a particular flower, one must first know the characteristics and form of the flower, then find a class in the schedule that would best show it off.

The Lily is a leafy-stemmed, erect, showy flower with a graceful form. A class that requires a free-form design would be a good choice in which to enter a design using this handsome flower. To add contrast to this upright flower, branches of Dogwood were used.

SUPPLIES

Container—Japanese low
rectangle
Needlepoint holder—
approximately 3″

PLANT MATERIAL

3 Lily stems with 3 flowers
and 5 buds
5 Dogwood branches

PROCEDURE

Place the needlepoint holder in the back left corner of the container.

Cut Dogwood branch #1 about two times the length of the container and place it to the left back on the needlepoint holder. It should bend gracefully toward the center.

Cut branch #2 so it will be long enough to extend beyond the side of the container and place it low and diagonally across from #1. Carefully trim side branches to help strengthen the look of the main line.

Cut branch #3 to fill in space on the left side of #1.

Cut branch #4 short and place it on right side of #1.

Cut branch #5 short and place it behind #1.

Use Lily stem #6 in the erect position. It should be cut shorter than the tallest Dogwood. Place it slightly to the right of the #1 branch.

Cut flower stem #7 slightly shorter than #6 and place it close to the right side of #6 slanting to the right.

Cut flower stem #8 shorter than #7 and place it close to #6 on the left side. If the flowers and buds seem to be crowded, carefully cut off some of them to improve the look of the design.

DEFINITION: A **free-form design** is a creative design that is free from conventional ideas and patterns, within the limits of the principles of design.

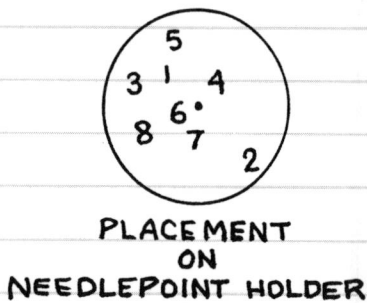

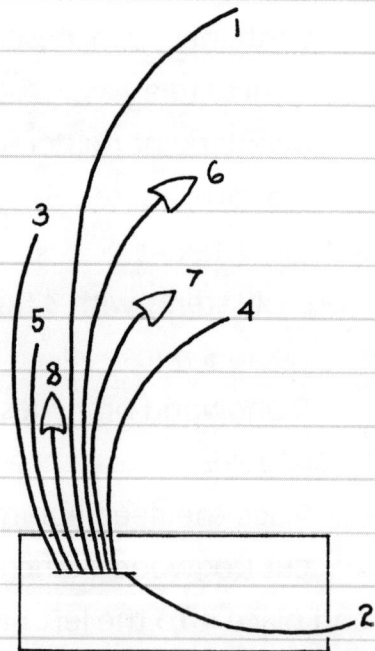

PLACEMENT
ON
NEEDLEPOINT HOLDER

DESIGN 12   BEGIN WITH A CONTAINER

Class 2. A dramatic design of all dried and treated dried plant material.

A large, black glass globe container meets one of the requirements of this class. The size and color of the container are dramatic; and the decision to use all white, or off-white, plant material added further excitement.

Lunaria is very easy to grow in the garden. When it reaches maturity, cut it and hang it upside down to dry. Bleached Teasels and Cane twists similar to those used in this design can be purchased wherever dried plant material is sold.

Because of the size and round shape of the container, a large mass of dried plant material was needed. No mechanics were necessary because the plant material supported itself and the opening in the container was small. The dried Teasels and Cane twists were very lightweight so they stayed in place when inserted in the Lunaria.

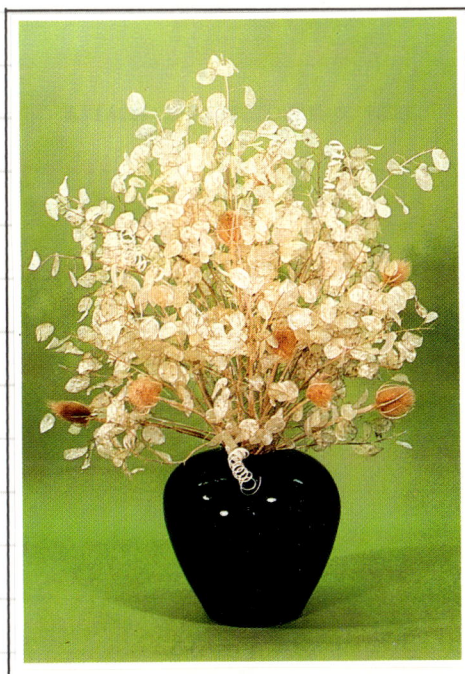

SUPPLIES

   Container—large, black glass
      globe, 12″ diameter

PLANT MATERIAL

   8 Lunaria stems—dried

   7 Teasels—bleached

   5 Cane twists

PREPARATION

To prepare the Lunaria, remove the outer coverings and seeds by twisting each floret gently between the thumb and first finger.

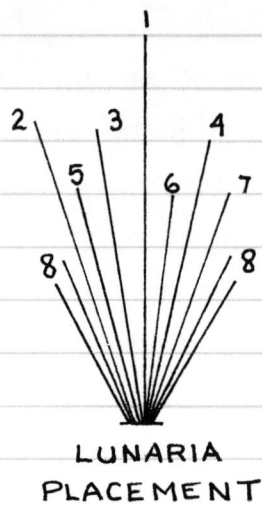

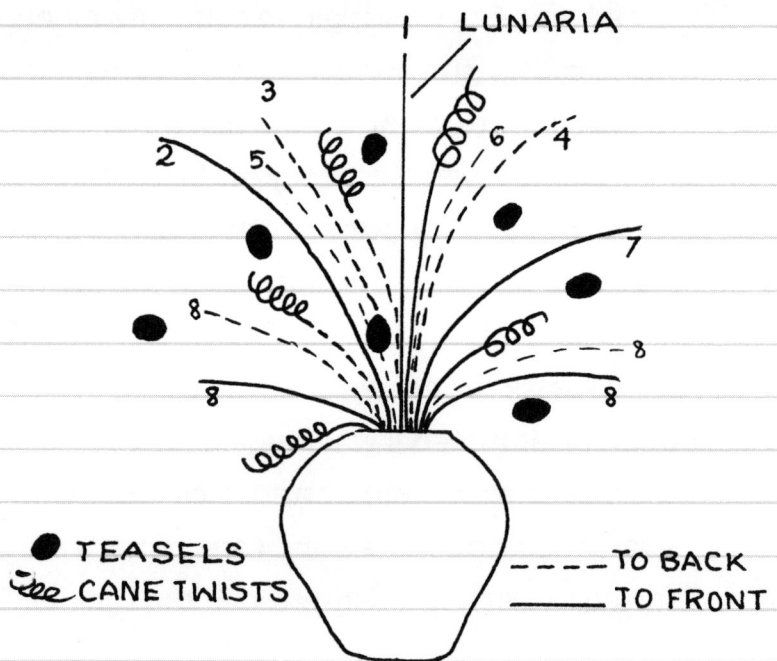

LUNARIA
PLACEMENT

LUNARIA

● TEASELS
〰 CANE TWISTS

- - - - TO BACK
———— TO FRONT

PROCEDURE

Select #1, the tallest Lunaria stem (approximately 40" tall), with all its branches attached, and place it in the center of the container. The bottom branches of the stem will rest on the rim of the container. They will act as a flower holder and support the remainer of the plant material.

In a very orderly manner, insert the next three, slightly shorter, Lunaria stems #2, #3, and #4 around #1.

Cut #5, #6, and #7 shorter than #2, #3, and #4, and place in between them. Lunaria #8 is cut into short pieces and each piece is inserted wherever needed to fill out the rounded mass shape.

Cut the Teasels and Cane twists to different lengths and insert them in the Lunaria.

Class 3. ROUND AND ROUND. A creative design featuring circles.

Fresh and treated dried plant material required.

The class title, "Round and Round," is the theme. Think of this and immediately circles come to mind. To carry out this idea, picture a round or circular container with circular plant material.

Plant material that bends easily can be used to make circles of different sizes; for example, fresh Jasmine, Pussy Willow, Weeping Willow, or Forsythia branches that have been stripped of all their foliage.

Since circles are to be featured, create a background of circles cut from matboard. Two pieces will be needed. Cut the largest circle possible from a piece of white matboard; then cut the circle in half and reverse the halves. Mount them on a piece of blue matboard using double-faced tape.

SUPPLIES

    Container—Japanese black circle

    Matboards—1 blue and 1 white,

      each 32″ by 40″

    Spray paint—flat black

    Balsa wood stick—1/2″ by 1/2″

      by 15″ long

PLANT MATERIAL

    35 Jasmine stems

    10 Euphorbia stems with orange

      flowers

PREPARATION

Cut 35 Jasmine stems, as long as possible. Strip off all the leaves. Make five groups of stems, having the same length stems in each group. Wire each group of stems together about 2" from the bottom. Group #1 has 7 stems; group #2 has 7; group #3 has 10; group #4 has 7; and group #5 has 4.

Bend the top of each group to make a different size circle. These circles should be made smaller than desired for the design. The tips may be bent around two or three times before wiring them together in two places. After the stems have dried and the wiring has been removed, the circles will expand. Stand the five groups of circles upright in an empty container until they are completely dry.

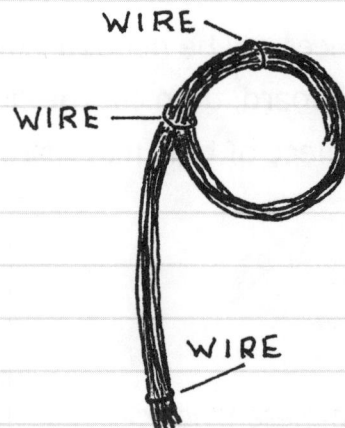

PROCEDURE

The height of the background will regulate the height of the finished design. Cut a 15″ length of 1/2″ by 1/2″ Balsa wood that will stand upright on the bottom of the container. Four groups of circles will be wired to this piece of wood. Square Balsa is used because its soft edges will help keep the wires in place. Wire would slip on a round hardwood dowel.

To keep each group of Jasmine stems together, wire around the bottom after it has been cut to the desired height, but before it is wired to the Balsa wood stick.

WIRED TO
TOP OF
WOOD

2
WIRED TO
FRONT OF
WOOD

3
WIRED TO
BACK OF
WOOD

4
WIRED TO
FRONT OF
WOOD

1 - STRAIGHT
UP

2 -
TO SIDE
FRONT

3 - TO BACK

4 - TO
SIDE
FRONT

WOOD
6 - FLOWERS

5 - TO CENTER
FRONT

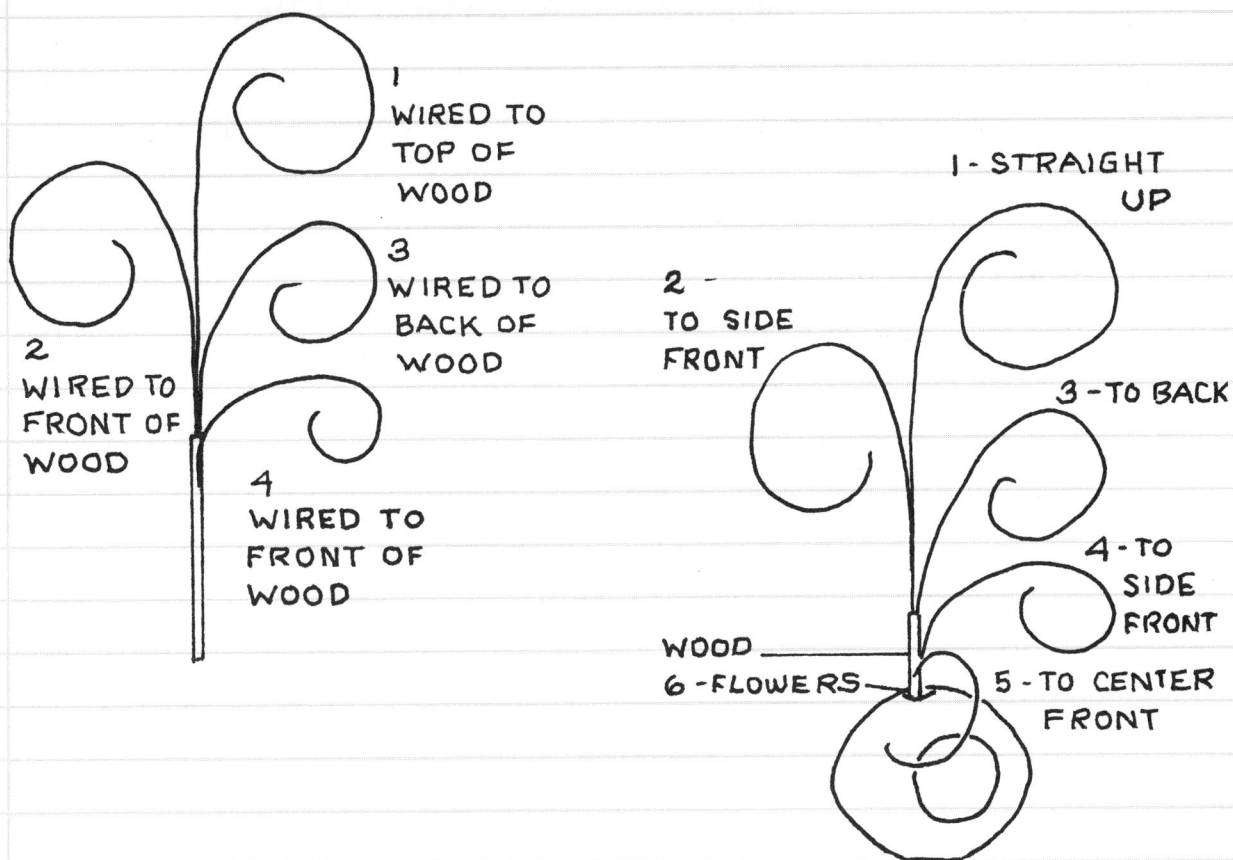

The largest circle, #1, has the longest stems and is placed at the top of the design. The next groups are slightly shorter with smaller circles.

Group #1 is wired to the top of the Balsa wood stick. Group #2 is wired to the front left side. Group #3 is wired to the right side and leans toward the back. Group #4 is wired lower on the Balsa stick and leans toward the front right side. Group #5 is not wired to the Balsa wood. Later it will be inserted low in the center front of the container leaning toward the right. But first, all of the circles and the Balsa wood stick should be sprayed with flat black paint. When completely dry, place them in the container.

To complete the design, arrange the Euphorbia stems, while holding them in one hand, so they hang like a bunch of grapes. Tie them together and place them so they hang over the rim of the container.

DEFINITION: A **feature** is anything that is dominant in a design. A feature may be any object, color, selected plant material, etc. Anything may be featured, but only when it dominates. In this design, circles are featured.

DESIGN 14   BEGIN WITH AN IDEA

Class 4. An abstract design using unusual and exotic plant material.

Anything can spark the imagination. Workmen taking down an old Sugar Maple tree finished digging out most of the roots, then left for the day. The sight of all those curving roots standing in the sunlight sparked the idea of using them in a flower design.

The container to show off the roots would have to be unusual. A very narrow Japanese container with six openings was selected. Its color, a mixture of beige and light brown, complemented the color of the roots.

One large exotic flower, or two, would complete the design—a large Protea with pink and brown edges, a large cluster of yellow or orange deciduous Azalea flowers, a colorful Rhododendron, a Magnolia blossom with its shiny leaves, or a Banksia flower.

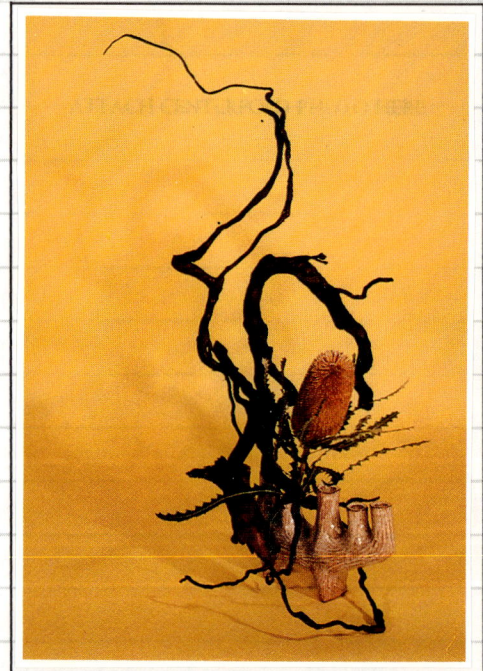

SUPPLIES

    Container—Japanese with six

      openings

    Shoe polish—brown liquid

PLANT MATERIAL

    2 Tree roots

    1 Banksia flower—large

PREPARATION

    Scrub the tree roots, using a wire brush and a garden hose. Trim off all the small rootlets. This strengthens the look of the main root. Let the roots dry for several days.

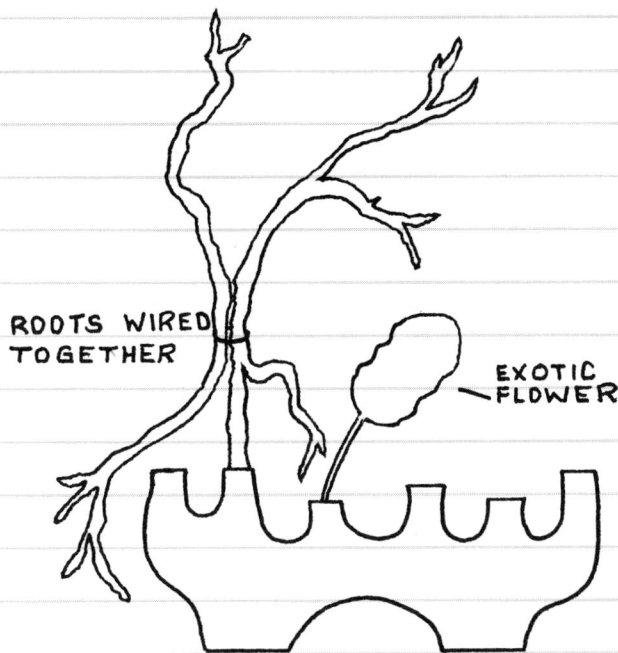

ROOTS WIRED
TOGETHER

EXOTIC
FLOWER

PROCEDURE

It may be necessary to wire two or more roots together to make an
interesting pattern. Place the root, or roots, in the container using only
one opening. More trimming may be necessary to strengthen the main line
of the roots. When the roots are arranged satisfactorily, remove them
from the container and paint them with brown liquid shoe polish. Let
them dry completely before replacing them in the container.

Place the large flower with a little of its foliage in the opening next to
the one holding the root. No mechanics are necessary because the openings of the container are small, and they will support the plant material.
Only two openings are used; the others are left empty.

DEFINITION: **Abstract design** is a creative art form in which plant material
and other components are used solely as line, form, color, and texture,
with space to create new images.

SECTION IV

DON'T SPARE THE FLOWERS

Little designs in multiple containers, grouped together, can make one overall design. The group becomes a decorative unit instead of one large centerpiece.

Grouping small flowers in a cluster of small containers gives maximum decoration with minimum plant material and expense. Each design can be different and can contain unlike flowers; however, all have to blend and complement each other. Position these small designs carefully to create overall harmony.

An endless number of ideas for special occasions or parties can be developed. For instance, for a bachelor party use a collection of antique bar glasses; for an African safari party use a collection of animal candlesticks with adaptors for flowers.

DESIGN 15   CONCH SHELL COLLECTION

Collecting seashells is a fascinating hobby because of the endless number of varieties, sizes, and colors. Conch shells can be grouped together as containers for flowers in a design to be used on a patio table in the summertime. Since outdoor dining is usually informal, informal flowers, such as daisies, are a good choice for the plant material.

In this design, seven shells were used. Three similar conch shells were placed together on the left side, one unusual and beautiful conch shell was placed in the center, and three more similar shells were grouped together on the right side. A chartreuse cloth was chosen because of its cool appearance and because it would highlight the effect of the white shells holding the daisies. A green-and-white color scheme could be used throughout the table setting—white flowers, green cloth, white china, green crystal.

SUPPLIES

    7 Conch shells

    Gesso paint—white

    6 Needlepoint holders—
       very small

    Floral foam

PLANT MATERIAL

    18 Daisies—white

PREPARATION

Select six conch shells that are the same size and shape, and one beautiful, unusual conch shell that is longer and more narrow than the six that are to be used as flower containers. Paint the outside of all the shells flat white using Gesso paint. Leave the inside of the shells the natural color.

Cut floral foam into six 1 1/2" cubes and soak the cubes in water until they are saturated.

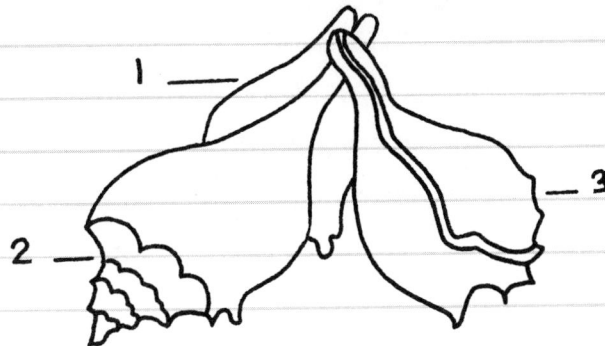

PROCEDURE

Hold three shells by their pointed ends and fit them together until they stand upright. If necessary to make them secure, use floral adhesive at the top where the three shells touch. Follow the same procedure with the other three shells. One group of shells is placed to the left and the other to the right of the odd shell. The single shell should rest diagonally between the two groups.

Remove the floral foam from the water and insert each piece onto a small needlepoint holder. Then insert one needlepoint holder with floral foam into the inside of each of the six shells. The floral foam will be held in place by the curved edges of the shell and will be weighted down by the small needlepoint holder.

Cut the Daisy stems about 6" long and insert three flowers into each shell in a triangular pattern. Use Daisy foliage to fill in empty spaces in each shell.

VARIATION: Place the shells in a diagonal line on the table.

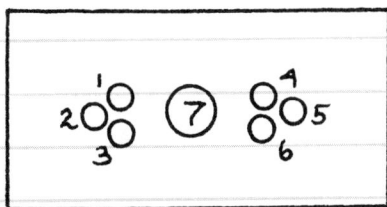

STRAIGHT PLACEMENT   DIAGONAL PLACEMENT

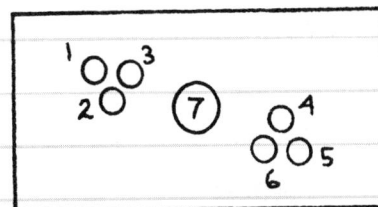

DESIGN 16   CRYSTAL COLLECTION

A combination of crystal can make an unusual design, full of sparkle, when placed on a mirror base. A base adds unity to a design.

It is important to use crystal of the same pattern. However, crystal of different sizes and shapes may be combined. For a tall design, crystal pieces may be stacked on top of each other by turning the bottom one upside down.

In this design two small bud vases were used as candle holders. Two kinds of flowers were used: Leptospermum, which has a spike form; and spray Carnations, which have a round form. A spike flower is a lengthened flower cluster in which the flowers are practically stemless. A spray flower always has a main stem with side branches and blooms on all stems. Sprays may be divided to make individual flowers and buds.

The completed design was not photographed on the mirror base because of distracting reflections; however, it is more dramatic when the base is used.

SUPPLIES

1 Waterford water goblet
1 Waterford wine glass
1 Waterford juice glass
2 Waterford bud vases
1 Mirror base
2 Candles—pink

PLANT MATERIAL

6 Sprays of pink Carnations
3 Leptospermum—pink
9 Boston fern

PREPARATION

Select three glasses of different sizes to make one design when placed together on a mirror base. It is important to work on all three designs at the same time. Work directly in front of the glasses, which should be placed in the position planned for the finished triple design. No mechanics will be needed because the Leptospermum will hold the flowers.

PROCEDURE

Cut the fullest piece of Leptospermum 8" long and place it in the center of the water goblet. Place a shorter piece of Leptospermum in the center of the wine glass. Place the shortest piece of Leptospermum in the center of the juice glass. Divide any remaining pieces of the Leptospermum among the three containers as needed to fill them.

CONTAINER 1—Water Goblet. Fill with 1/2 of the small pink Carnations and 1/3 of the Fern. The design must be finished on all sides.

CONTAINER 2—Wine Glass. Place wine glass to the left front of the water goblet. Fill with 1/4 of the small pink Carnations and 1/3 of the fern. The right back of this design should not be as full as Container 1.

CONTAINER 3—Juice Glass. Place the juice glass to the right of Container 1 and slightly forward of Container 2. Fill with 1/4 of the small pink Carnations and 1/3 of the Fern. The left back of this design should not be as full as Container 1.

Place additional Fern in all three designs wherever needed to give a graceful look.

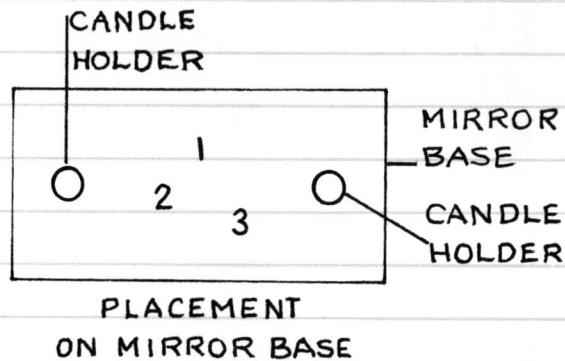

PLACEMENT
ON MIRROR BASE

Place the three containers in the center of the mirror base with the water goblet slightly to back, the wine glass on the left side, and the juice glass to the right front.

Insert the pink candles in the bud vases and place on each side of the triple design.

DESIGN 17   RICE BOWL COLLECTION

Oriental rice bowls make delightful and attractive containers when stacked. To make a group of them look like a single design, use a base such as a black lacquer disc or a gold tray turned upside down to show its black underside. The color of the bowls or the decorations on the bowls should be a guide to the color and type of flowers and foliage to be used.

One attractive combination of plant material for black-and-white bowls would be salmon-colored Shrimp Plant flowers and foliage, used with sprigs of Privet hedge with black berries, and curls of black rubber-covered wire.

At a different season of the year, yellow Freesia and Fern could be used. Small spray Carnations and Miniature Roses would be a good choice because of their lovely colors and petite size.

SUPPLIES

    7 Rice bowls

    Wire, black rubber-covered—

       5″ long

    3 Needlepoint holders—

       2″ diameter

    Floral adhesive—white

    Disc—black-lacquer

PLANT MATERIAL

    11 Freesia flowers—yellow

    3 Baker fern

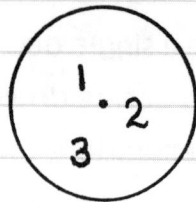

PLACEMENT
OF
CONTAINERS

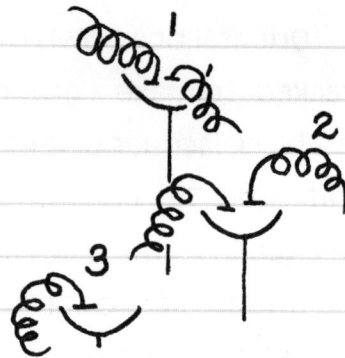

PLACEMENT OF SPIRALS

PREPARATION

Make three containers out of seven rice bowls.

CONTAINER 1—Use four bowls and secure them together with floral adhesive. Start by turning the bottom bowl upside down and work up, alternating the bowls.

CONTAINER 2—Use two bowls for the second container. Start with the bottom bowl turned upside down. Place the second bowl on top, right side up.

CONTAINER 3—A single bowl is used for the third container.

PROCEDURE

With floral clay, secure a small needlepoint holder in each container, and place the containers on the black lacquer disc.

Cut the black wire into five pieces, each 12″ long. Wind each piece of wire around the handle of a wooden spoon to make a spiral, leaving a 2″ straight piece of wire on the end. Pull the spoon handle out of the wire spiral. Place two spirals each in Containers 1 and 2, and one in Container 3. The black spirals should be placed so they arch toward each other throughout the entire design. The three containers make a single design.

Place five flowers in Container 1 so they look toward Container 2. The four flowers in Container 2 should look toward Container 3, which should have two flowers.

Cut the Baker fern into five or six pieces, placing the largest piece in Container 1. The next largest piece of fern goes in Container 2, and the shortest piece goes into Container 3. Fill in where necessary with remaining small pieces of fern.

PLACEMENT OF PLANT MATERIAL

DESIGN 18   CRANBERRY GLASS COLLECTION

After years of collecting a particular kind of glass, it is rewarding to be able to use some of the collection for a flower design on the dining room table during the Christmas season.

A bottle, a cruet, and a small pitcher of cranberry glass were grouped with two flower designs in containers fashioned from other pieces in the collection, to form a decorative unit. For dramatic effect, a double design was created for a table set with a cranberry-color linen cloth underneath an ecru lace cloth. Cranberry linen napkins were also used along with cranberry glass goblets and wine glasses. For a dinner table, brass candlesticks with cranberry candles could be used.

For the photograph, the bottle, cruet, and small pitcher were pulled about two inches away from the flower design.

SUPPLIES
- 1 Candlestick with a bobeche
- 1 Round bowl
- 1 Flair compote
- 1 Bottle
- 1 Cruet
- 1 Pitcher
- 2 Needlepoint holders—
  - 2″ diameter

PLANT MATERIAL
- 6 Alstroemeria—red
- 3 Leptospermum—red

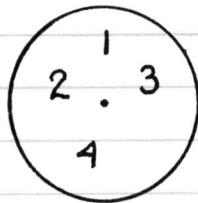

PLACEMENT
ON
NEEDLEPOINT
HOLDERS

1

2

PROCEDURE

Work on both flower designs at the same time. Use floral clay to secure the needlepoint holders in the small bowl and the flair compote. Place the bowl on top of the candlestick. A bobeche may be added to the candle-stick, if it does not have a wide flange, to hold the bowl in place. Or floral clay could be used to hold the candlestick and bowl together. The height of the design is determined by the height of the first piece of Leptosper-mum. Select a full, graceful stem for the first placement.

CONTAINER 1—#1 Leptospermum is 10″ long and placed to the center back.

> #2 Alstroemeria is 7″ long and placed slightly forward and to the left of #1.

> #3 Alstroemeria is 6″ long and placed slightly forward and to the right of #1.

> #4 Alstroemeria is 5″ long and placed in the center front. If the design is not full enough, insert small pieces of Lep-tospermum where needed.

CONTAINER 2—The placement of the plant material is exactly the same as in Container 1. The only difference is that the plant material is all cut shorter.

#1 Leptospermum is 7″ long and placed to the center back.

#2 Alstroemeria is 5″ long and placed slightly forward and to the left of #1.

#3 Alstroemeria is 4″ long and placed slightly forward and to the right of #1.

#4 Alstroemeria is 3″ long and placed in the center front. If needed, fill in the design with additional very short pieces of Leptospermum.

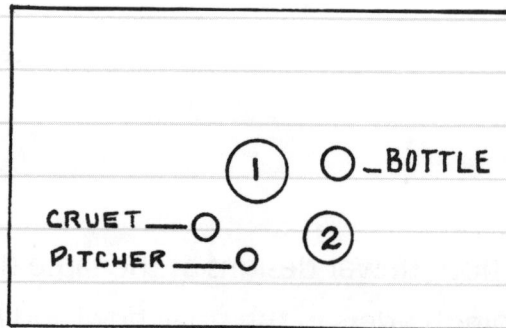

PLACEMENT OF UNITS

Place Container 1, the candlestick with the bowl on top, in the center of the table. Container 2, the flair compote, is placed to the right of Container 1. The cruet is placed close to left front side of Container 1. The pitcher is placed to the left side of Container 2. The bottle is placed to the right center of Container 1 and the center back of Container 2.

SECTION V

QUICKIE FLOWER DESIGNS

These quickie flower designs are presented with the hope that they will give confidence to beginners when cutting plant material. Novices are sometimes afraid to cut flower stems and branches for they know that once a stem has been cut it cannot be put back together. However, if a new flower arranger has one diagram to follow for cutting and another one for placing the plant material in a needlepoint holder, fear is overcome and a well-organized flower design is the outcome.

Filler plant material is transitional plant material of various lengths that is used to fill between the stems of the main plant material; for example, fern or foliage. After placing the primary flowers and branches in a needlepoint holder, filler foliage may be added.

The height of a flower design is based on many factors. In the home, location and function are the most important factors. For instance, a table centerpiece for a seated meal requires a design that is low enough to allow the guests to see over it, but a buffet table needs a taller design.

For a flower show, the height of a design is controlled by the schedule, the height of the background, and the type of design; for example, a vertical design must be tall, but a horizontal design must be low and wide. In many Oriental designs, the size of the container regulates the height of the plant material; that is, the height of the first placement is at least one and one half times the width or height of the container, whichever is the largest dimension.

A QUICK AND EASY METHOD FOR CUTTING FLOWERS

1. Line up flowers on a table in an orderly manner, according to the diagrams for the designs in this section.

2. Start with the tallest and proceed to the shortest.

3. Place the first flower, with flower head at the desired height for the design, with the end of the stem extending over the table edge.

4. Proceed in the same manner with each succeeding flower, according to the diagrams.

5. After all the flowers are lined up, cut off the stems even with the table edge.

6. Strip off all the leaves that will be under water.

7. Place the flowers on the needlepoint holder according to the numbers in the diagrams.

8. Add some filler plant material to fill in the spaces between the main lines of the design.

DESIGN 19   MASS—START WITH NINE FLOWERS

Start with nine flowers and filler plant material. Place needlepoint holder in the center of the container.

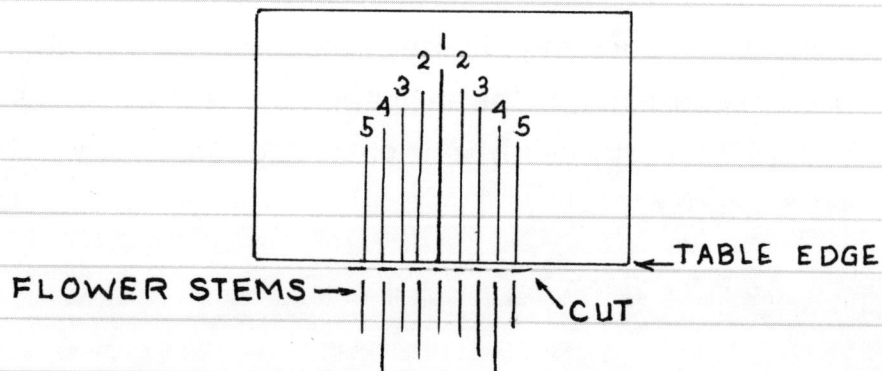

SUPPLIES

    Oval container

    Needlepoint holder—3″

      or 4″ diameter

PLANT MATERIAL

    9 Flowers

    10 to 12 Baker fern

PROCEDURE

    Place needlepoint holder in the center of the container.

    Place #1 flower in the center of needlepoint.

    Place the two #2's low and to each side. Part of each flower should extend over the edge of the container.

    Place the two #3's slightly higher, one to the front and one to the back.

    Place the two #4's higher in the same manner as the #3's, one to the front and one to the back.

    Place the two #5's in front and in back of #1, with part of each flower extending over the edge of the container.

    Place filler foliage under #1 and throughout the design, leaning in the same direction as the flowers but always shorter.

    Always work alternating from front to back. This will make the design the same on each side. Flowers should be only slightly different in length. They appear to be different because of the angles at which they are placed.

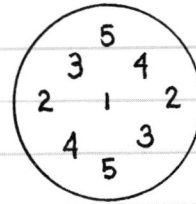

PLACEMENT
ON
NEEDLE POINT HOLDER

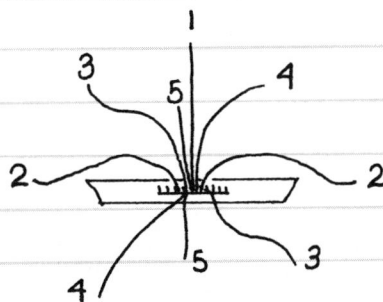

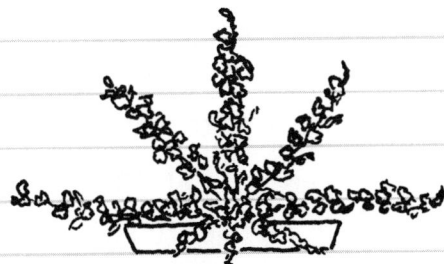

DESIGN 20   VERTICAL—START WITH FIVE FLOWERS

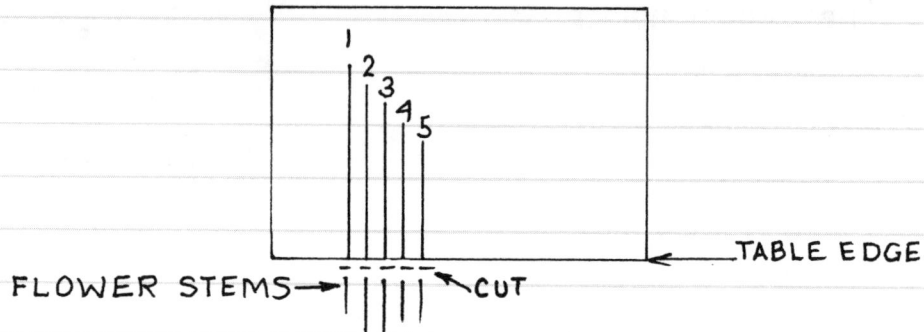

FLOWER STEMS →

CUT

TABLE EDGE

SUPPLIES

Container—small

Needlepoint holder—3″ diameter

PLANT MATERIAL

5 Tall straight flowers—Gladiolus,

Delphiniums, Snapdragons

Filler foliage—Lemon Leaf sprays

or Baker fern

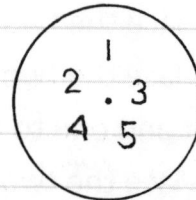

PLACEMENT
ON
NEEDLEPOINT HOLDER

PROCEDURE

Place needlepoint in center back of container. Place #1 flower in center back of needlepoint. Work from the back to the front, cutting each flower shorter than the preceding one. This is called the "shoe lacing" method of placing plant material on the needlepoint holder.

Place #2 to left of #1 and slightly forward.

Place #3 to right of #1 and slightly forward of #2.

Place #4 to left front between #1 and #2.

Place #5 to right front of #3.

Place filler foliage around the flower stems. Place the tallest piece of foliage on the left side and the shortest piece coming partly over the right side of the container. A piece of foliage may go in back.

NOTE: Always exaggerate the height of plant material in a vertical design.

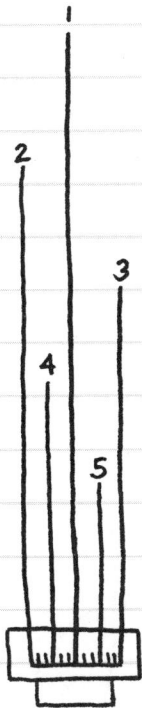

PLACEMENT
OF
FLOWERS

PLACEMENT
OF
FOLIAGE

DESIGN 21   ORIENTAL MANNER—START WITH THREE BRANCHES, TWO FLOWERS, AND THREE LEAVES

SUPPLIES

    Container—round

    Needlepoint holder—3″ diameter

PLANT MATERIAL

    3 Branches—either bare or flowering

    2 Flowers

    3 Leaves

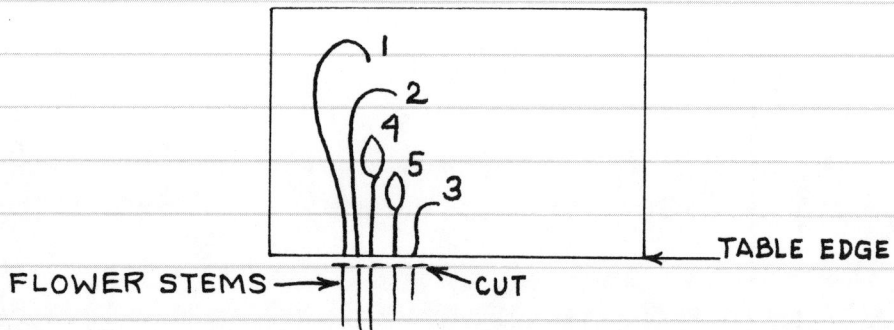

FLOWER STEMS →   ← CUT   TABLE EDGE

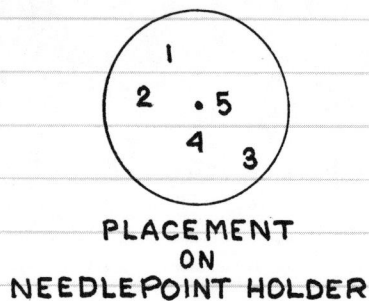

PLACEMENT
ON
NEEDLEPOINT HOLDER

PROCEDURE

    Place needlepoint holder in the left back of the container.

    Cut #1 branch at least two times the diameter of the container. Place this branch to left back on the needlepoint.

    Cut #2 branch 3/4 the length of #1 and place it to the left front of #1.

66

Cut #3 branch 3/4 of #2 and place it very low leaning to the right front.

Place #4 flower in the center of the needlepoint and lean it slightly forward.

Place #5 flower in the back and to the right of #4. Lean it in the same direction as #4.

Place the 3 leaves so they follow the same direction as the flowers.

DESIGN 22   FREE STYLE—START WITH A MIXTURE OF FLOWERS
AND FOLIAGE

SUPPLIES

    Container—tall cylinder

PLANT MATERIAL

    A bunch of mixed flowers

      and foliage

PROCEDURE

    Strip the leaves from the bottom third of the stems.

    Pick up the flowers and foliage, one at a time, holding them together in one hand.

    Rotate the flowers as additional ones are added. Remember to mix and blend flowers, colors, and foliage.

    Tie the stems together with a piece of raffia or string at the point where they were held.

    Cut the stems evenly across the bottom.

    Place in a tall cylindrical container or vase. Branches resting on rim of container will hold flowers in place. Tied area should fall below rim of container.

NOTE: A **free style design** is a naturalistic one, using plant material as it grows in nature.

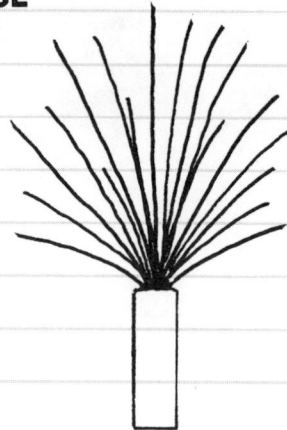

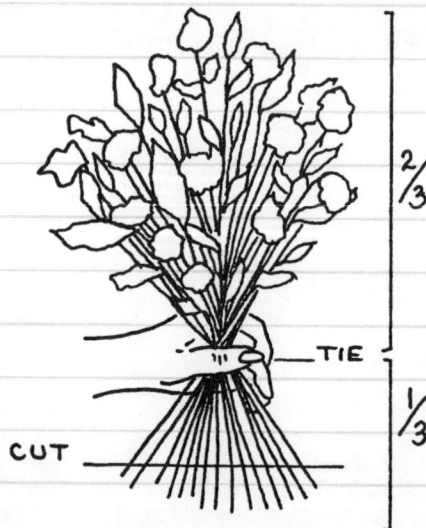

68

DESIGN 23   CASUAL DESIGN—START WITH A HANDFUL
OF FLOWERS

SUPPLIES

Container—cylinder

PLANT MATERIAL

A handful of flowers that are all

the same variety—Daisies,

Violets, Zinnias, or Marigolds.

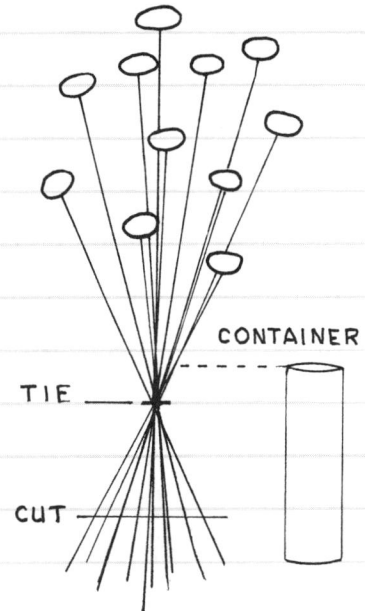

PROCEDURE

Hold all the flowers loosely in one hand with all the flower heads at the same height. Start by pulling the center flower up, then pull the surrounding flowers upward, but always slightly lower than the center flower.

Keep turning the flowers, pulling upward and outward, always working in a circle.

Tie with raffia or string at the point where the flowers were held in hand.

Strip off all leaves that will be under water.

Cut off the stems evenly on the bottom.

Place in cylindrical container. The container can be any height from one inch to eight inches, depending upon the flowers; for example, Violets would be placed in a two-inch container, and Zinnias would be placed in an eight-inch container.

DESIGN 24   CRYSTAL VASE—START WITH A NANDINA BRANCH
USED AS A FLOWER HOLDER

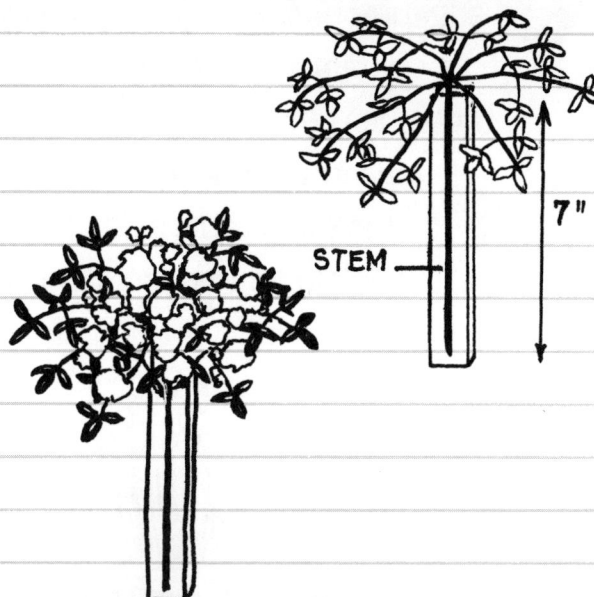

SUPPLIES

Container—Crystal vase, about
7 inches tall

PLANT MATERIAL

1 Nandina branch

6 Sprays of small Carnations,
Daisies, or Chrysanthemums

PROCEDURE

Because of its shape, a Nandina branch will make a good holder for flowers that have slender stems. Select a branch that has a small well-shaped circular top with all the leaflet branches radiating outward from the main stem. Remove all lower branches on the main stem keeping only the umbrella-like top. Cut the branch so the base of the branch can rest on the bottom of the container, with the circular leaflet branches resting on the rim.

The flower sprays may be cut into single flowers and buds, or they may be used as sprays. Strip off all leaves that will be under water. Since the stems will be seen through the crystal vase, they should be placed in an orderly fashion in the Nandina branch. The result should be a mound of flowers with the center slightly raised and each flower placed slightly lower than the preceding one—and all supported by the Nandina branch.

This is an excellent design for a coffee table. When looking down on the design, the Nandina leaves should extend three or four inches beyond the flowers. They may have to be trimmed.

VARIATION: Several sprays of small-leaf Holly or Cotoneaster may be used in place of the Nandina—with small red Carnations.

70

GLOSSARY

ABSTRACT DESIGN—a creative art form in which plant material and other components are used solely as line, form, color, and texture with space to create new images.

ACCESSORY—anything subordinate, extra, added, or helping in a secondary way. It is an optional component of an arrangement, being anything in addition to plant material, container, base, or background.

ASYMMETRICAL BALANCE—approximate equal visual weight composed of different elements on each side of an imaginary vertical axis. Balance without symmetry.

BALANCE—visual stability.

COMPONENTS—physical material of which an arrangement is composed; that is, plant material, container, background, and mechanics.

CONDITIONING—preparation of cut plant material before arranging.

CREATIVITY—an original concept in the choice of components or in the organization of the design elements within the limitations of the principles of design.

DECORATIVE UNIT—consists of either one or more flower arrangements, or the arrangements plus accessories.

DESIGN ATTRIBUTES—beauty, harmony, distinction, and expression.

DESIGN ELEMENTS—the basic visual qualitites of a design—space, line, form, size, color, texture, pattern, and light.

DESIGN PRINCIPLES—basic art standards used to organize design elements—balance, proportion, scale, rhythm, dominance, and contrast.

DRIED PLANT MATERIAL—plant material from which the moisture has been removed.

DRIFTWOOD—that which has been washed by the ocean, lake, or stream.

EXHIBITION TABLE—table which is not related to function.

FILLER PLANT MATERIAL—transitional plant material used to fill in between different plant forms.

FLOWER ARRANGING—the art of organizing the design elements of plant material and other components according to design principles to obtain beauty, harmony, distinction, and expression.

FREE STANDING—a design to be viewed from all sides.

FRESH PLANT MATERIAL—any part severed from a living plant, in fresh condition.

GRADATION—a sequence in which there is regular and orderly change in size, form, color, or texture.

GROOMING—cleaning flowers to remove dirt and spray residue as well as dead or broken foliage or flowers.

HARDENING—to place plant material in water several hours before arranging.

LIGHT—illumination, either natural or artificial, that is necessary for vision. A design element, it relates to design by affecting color, shadow, and visibility of an exhibit.

MECHANICS—contrivances used to hold and control materials in design.

MOBILE—a grouping of suspended forms having visual balance in which actual movement can be induced by air currents.

NATURALISTIC—using plant material as it grows.

SYMMETRICAL BALANCE—similar on two sides of a real or imaginary vertical axis.

TREATED DRIED PLANT MATERIAL—plant material that has had the surface texture, color, or substance changed, yet is still recognizable as plant material. The change is effected by application of any substance or agent such as wax, dye, paint, shellac, or the plant material may be glycerinized, skeletonized, or bleached.

WEATHERED WOOD—that which has been exposed to the weather; namely, sun, rain,and wind.

With appreciation to the National Council of State Garden Clubs, Inc., for permission to use selected definitions from its *Handbook for Flower Shows.*